Joseph Rocchietti

Charles Rovellini

A Drama of the Disunited States of North America

Joseph Rocchietti

Charles Rovellini
A Drama of the Disunited States of North America

ISBN/EAN: 9783337336844

Printed in Europe, USA, Canada, Australia, Japan

Cover: Foto ©Thomas Meinert / pixelio.de

More available books at **www.hansebooks.com**

CHARLES ROVELLINI

A DRAMA

OF THE

DISUNITED STATES OF NORTH AMERICA

BY

JOSEPH ROCCHIETTI

FROM

CASALE MONFERRATO

I LOVE thee not, and this thou knowest; thou
Who lov'st not Rome, sole cause I do not love thee:
I do not envy thee, because no more
I deem myself inferior to thyself:
I do not fear thee, Cæsar, since I'm always
Ready to die rather than be a slave;
And, finally, I hate thee not, because
In nothing do I fear thee. Now then hear
Brutus alone; to him alone yield faith.
                              VICTOR ALFIERI.
         Translated by Charles Lloyd.

NEW-YORK
1875

JOHN AND CHARLES

WHO denies their rights to the people ?
The property-holders, the priests, the nobles, and the king.

L. MÜHLBACH.

YOUR death prostrated me with sorrow. The will of God be done. To you I dedicate this drama. Instead of lavishing their thoughts and the wealth of the nation with so many churches, had the Americans built houses for the poor, employed healthy, strong men to work for the benefit of the public, encouraged political economy, and placed into universities honorable professors of sciences and arts, this civil war would never have taken place. In heaven, my boys, you want no instruction from me now. What I am going to say, is with the intention to give an honest idea of true religion to your living brothers and my beloved Americans.

The so-called religious individual, telling to his citizens that, during this mortal life, we must think of nothing else but of the eternal one to come, and permit the devils to govern this temporal power, not to be compared, as he says, with the spiritual enjoyments—such a priest. is a traitor to his country. In taking you from your most sacred duty, and from the laws of your country, he keeps you to suffer the life of an ignorant monk, in order to fatten himself at the table of his bishop. Priestcraft, being catholic or reformed, has always inculcated hierarchies on earth and in heaven. Popes had Jesuits, monks, and nuns. When B. Franklin was living in Philadelphia, he left the church, in which he found the preachers always asking money instead of preaching morals. If, at that time, one of the noble fathers of this republic was thus writing in his life, what will we say now, that reverends hold many offices of our government ?

As the laws of nature are those of God, our best prayer should be the study of natural sciences, and the glory of progress. In placing you in His beautiful creation, and having given you mind and senses, God never intended to instruct you as your schoolteacher does. In His Divine silence, God teaches you, nights and days. The infinity of solar systems is a miracle which does not require other miracles. Without the work of man, the earth would be a sad wilderness of animals, eating each other, without law but that of the stronger ; therefore, our best prayer is for us to study and to work.

The books of Moses seem to have been written by other writers before him. This legislator, although he was a man of a great mind, his laws are not of God. The Creator, being perfect, could not be imperfect in his language, nor a tyrant to the Israelites and to other nations of His creation.

Infernal, theologian rulers left to us the histories of seven thousand years. Not only millions of innocent and better educated nations than their conquerors must have been annihilated ; their historical records must have been burned, as we know the burned library of Alexandria, sciences and arts. We, the posterity of those selfish rulers, we rue the great loss of the past ages' progress ! The selfish monsters exterminated, even, the memory or records of those unfortunate nations ! And such tyrannical vandalism was perpetrated for wishing to appear, themselves, the first legislators to their posterity ! And forced their children to believe, they had spoken, face to face, with God ! Hence, was originated Theocracy, Monarchy, and Despotism. The democratic or republican government, being the only government for which God created mankind, it will never reach its perfection but from the true philosophy of man, free from all religious priestcraft.

The only monuments of Central America tell us of nations whose generations must have been extinguished. The infinity of solar systems, do they not tell us that this world had no beginning ? Had He lived in darkness during his first eternity, God could not be God. We can conceive our souls still existing into more subtile matter, but the Eternal Spirit, out of his creation, is an absurdity. To compare God and his creation with us, poor ephemeral insects, is nothing else but the foolish comparison of preachers with the chronometer and the watch-maker.

Infinity has no end ; like the number, it is space added to space, as eternity is time added to time. A certain space, or a certain time, have a beginning and an end. In the infinite space we may imagine a centre at every point, and in eternity, at every time, we can imagine the middle of the first and second eternities. During the first eternity, I know that my individuality was nothing, although I know, that my body and mind have been formed from the eternal elements or molecules. The annihilation of our soul, being too painful to me, my hope of the eternal future life is a great consolation for me on this mortal planet. But this divine consolation is perverted and taken from me, and from the hope of students, by ignorant and wily priests blessing *the poor of mind and cursing the students of nature.*

The democratic or republican government, the people's government, free of all priestcrafts, is the only good one for which

God created us. The republics of Athens, Sparta, and Rome had a religion which did not meddle with the grandeur of their temporal power. On the contrary, Minerva was the goddess of wisdom and liberty. Since our Christianity, not one single republic had been worthy to be compared with those of Greece and ancient Rome. The eternal hell creates slaves !

The fathers of this American Constitution, knowing such evils done by the church of the middle age in Italy, they provided laws against mischievous reverend doctors. Had they created censors, like Cato, to watch the morals and church's foxes, the country could not be now ruined. These fanatic Puritans, were they not the sons of the same Tories who burned alive innocent women as witches, one hundred years ago ?

Like Socrates, Jesus was a great Reformer. He called the Jews *vipers and hypocrites.* The meek teacher of peace could not suffer the warlike God of the Bible. Excepting the generals defending their country from tyranny, all unjust men of war are nothing else but robbers and assassins. Jesus had never said he was the only begotten Son of God. We are all sons and daughters of God. Priestcraft perverted his life. If the miracle of this world requires other miracles for our instruction, God would send a Jesus among every generation of man. His eternal justice would not have permitted him to send his Son God, only once forever into Jerusalem. All the nations of this weeping earth would have been equally provided. When Pope Sixtus saw his Catholics out of their wit, praying before a Christ shedding tears, he went to it with a hammer and broke the sculptured head. Two branches of a vine were fixed in each eye, protruding from a garden into the occiput of the Christ. It was during spring-time, when the vines are lopped. Such miraculous deceits, are they not discovered in our times also ? Many like rogues, did they not fatten themselves on such credulities ?

The money spent in America for printed Bibles and missionaries is incalculable. What have they done with it? Blood shed and mischief-makings to force angels to weep ! Not only Catholics and Reformers injure the morality of Jesus, and telling us of having said, "That no man can enter the kingdom of God, unless he be baptized ;" such a precept is a blasphemy ! It has a tendency to change Christians into ignorant slaves. Such a belief does not permit freedom to the human thought. Citizens, in such trammels, become monks, nuns, brutes, disregarding temporal instruction, for the so-called eternal glory in heaven ; and, by consequence, unfit to defend their temporal self-government. They are happy to die under the sword of their enemies ; they would not kill the enemy of their country, for the very reason that their country is in heaven without man's blood on their bands. But the duty of the citizen is to defend the rights of his country.

Among so many religions on the earth, few of them have been tolerant toward secular literature and professors of science. It seems to me the adorers of the Sun must have been a tolerant sect; but the crimes of innumerable sectarians form the sorrow of humanity! Besides the Jews, Pagans sacrificed human beings. In order to appease the anger of God, priests say: It was imperatively necessary to nail Jesus on the cross to save mankind. Such disgusting anger of the Father, is it not contradicting the peaceful character of the Son? And because my foe did injure me, my innocent son must be sacrificed? Our civil laws are better than the laws of the Christian God. We would hang such a father. This very foolish doctrine blinded and dragged the Americans to this civil war. How can we govern ourselves on earth, my boys, with good, civil, just laws, when a perverted religion teaches us injustice, cruelty, and excites us to an ungovernable passion? Such Christians, have they not roasted philosophers alive? Crimes, are they not originated from ignorance? Can man understand logic with a religion contradicting logic? Is God a cruel, intolerant monk?

If philosophers have contradicted your superstition, not one man of science has killed you, as you did them, with axes and fire. God has always left us free, without his intervention. Were He meddling himself in this temporal life, we would be all angels without popes nor rev. doctors; and when, instead of praying, all men will work and study God, then, and only then, we will enjoy Eden on this mortal earth. God had never meddled in religious slaughters, nor of kings' wars; the *Te Deum Laudamus*, on gained battles, are blasphemies! When we will have learned how to be dutiful children of God, without superstition, the future republics of our posterity will be, by far, more glorious than those of Athens, Sparta, and Rome.

The Pagans, as many other religions, have been suppressed with the progress of temporal wisdom. The Buddhists, Brahmans, Veda, and many other creeds, impossible to be enumerated, do they not prove they have not been originated by the same God? The Catholics are now divided into two creeds; and the Reformers, like the languages of Babel, have so many divisions, for which the human understanding is nothing better than the unfortunate talkings of mad-houses! And the poor suffering insanes say, that their own religion is the best. We have in some towns so many churches, for which the inhabitants are in despair how to get along, and for which the poor are left unprovided. It is only the men of science, who understand each other without contradiction, because they hold the true religion of God. The Zend-Avesta is the Bible of the Parsees; if the Jewish Bible is the law of God, the Gospel, so much differing from Moses' Bible, can not be the laws of God also ; or if the peaceful Jesus was the Son of God, the passionate Moses could not be the Man of God. I am inclined to believe that if the morals of the Gospel are better than the morals of the Old Testament, we are indebted to the progress of temporal science : and Socrates and Jesus were Reformers, after the philosophy of Plato.

We have, and we had, rabbins and ministers of the Gospel, whom we must respect as angels on earth. They are good, because they had the fortune of being better educated and instructed by a Savonarola, Bruno, or a Newton. Such religious men, such ministers of God, instead of calling Epicurus or Lucretius atheists with contempt, and sending these great men to hell, they have learned, from such original thinkers, the great charity of God, who, for our conservation,told us that self-love is the spring of motion and friendship. This natural gift in such original thinkers, not having changed it in selfishness, they act on earth like Socrates or Jesus Christ. The bad laws of man could not change their natural good heart. Such blessed ministers, being Turks, Jews, or Christians, form the honor and glory of our race. Oh! posterity, without the fear of intolerant churches, will enjoy the long time-expected millennium!

Citizens of America, Europe, Africa, New-Holland, Asia, we are all children of God. The universe is the worshiping temple of us all. Our churches are the public parks, fields, mountains, universities, theatres, colleges, libraries, and all schools of languages, mechanism, arts, and sciences. Our religious ministers should be the professors and teachers paid by our blessed government, when it will be blessed. From our public specula, we will learn how to glory and become good children of God, the Almighty of those infinite solar systems. It is of no use to ask of God to make us better men than we are. Since he wishes us to learn, and become better by the study of His sublime, perfect creation, so that our best prayer should be to instruct ourselves. When we will understand astronomy, then we will fall on our knees and say: "Oh ! this admirable world proclaims Thy glory!" It is not a long, sleepy prayer, which can unite us to God. Without the intelligence of a Newton, we will never understand the Almighty. Do you think that this wonderful world was created for slaves, brutes, or monks ? No man who did understand the sciences of God has ever been a criminal. Ignorance is our original sin. Priestcraft wants sinners. Without sinners, hypocrites could not pocket ten thousand dollars a year, and rent or lease the pews to rich people. A sectarian preacher may be eloquent for communities who do not understand logic nor mathematics ; but such Rev. Doctors, not knowing the sciences of God, are the very impostors who keep nations in bonds! Abolish wars, martial courts, church courts. The laws of our land should be only the civil courts, without capital penalty. During their youth, do not permit your children to smoke, nor to drink spirits. Punish the drunkards ; but leave free the adults and old people, to enjoy the temperate blessings of eating and drinking. Swearing, particularly in courts of justice, should be abolished. A simple lie is already a perjury. With the natural religion of God, we can not be afraid to present ourselves before the Eternal Throne.

JOSEPH ROCCHIETTI,
Linden, Union County,
New-Jersey.

PREFACE.

"Opus agredior opimum casibus, atrox prœliis, discors seditionibus, ipsa etiam pace sœvum."—TACITUS.

ON the first of 1845, fifteen years before our civil war, I published a pamphlet with which I demonstrated: *Why a National Literature can not flourish in the United States of North America.* Among the many truths which I published on that occasion, I said: "That we were at the eve *of a civil war!*" Some newspapers honored me with praises, and sinful, Whig editors ridiculed me and my pamphlet. The *Evening Post* and the *Herald* of New-York commended my honest work ; but among those who understood what literature is, and those who did not, I did not find one of them who could or would believe that we were at the *eve of a civil war in America.* Some called me a false prophet ; and the most polite ones to me said : that I, being not born in America, could not understand the parties of this republic, and that time would prove me wrong. I think a foreigner, acquainted with the language, is more qualified to judge of a nation in which he was not born than a native. But how can we have faith in man, while the very ones who called me a false prophet, during the civil war they had the impudence to tell to me that they knew, as well as myself, that we would have had the civil war ?

From the day in which Abraham Lincoln placed his feet on the presidential chair, we have now passed another course of fifteen years. Linden, Union County, New-Jersey, was the place in which I lived, as it is yet my place in which I live. Having always been a Democrat, fifteen years ago I said to the Democrats of my township : "That, if we were permitting Lincoln and his Whig party to wage war into the seceding or Confederate States, the Southerners, as well as the Northern States, would have been ruined, and our liberty gone forever." Scribblers and talkers might rob us still more of our money and build other monuments to Lincoln, but they can not force into the mind of the American people that the Republican party in 1875, time in which even the ignorant feel the smart of their wounds, that the Republicans are an honest party. The Republicans may praise themselves, boast of their war, cannons, assassinations, tortures, incendiaries, rapes, and all their roguish crimes perpetrated in the South and North of this weeping country, which are now authorized by infernal reverends, like dissolute, debauched Beechers, in the temples of Jesus. . . . The Republicans may praise themselves for having changed this Republic of Washington into their hell, but the honest Irish say, *self praise is no praise.* The honest Democrat does not deny that among Democrats we had rogues who called themselves Democrats, in order to cheat the people with a false name. But the war has taken off the masks from the faces of false Democrats, and the Republicans can not now mitigate their infernal deeds, because Tweed and other like war Democrats became slaves of Lincoln and party, to ruin this once blessed country.

That the judgment of man is perverted, we have only to study the history. Not with the mind of hypocrites. The people will never understand God as long as superstition, intolerance, in a word ; priestcraft of any denomination does not permit natural science to unmask popes, bishops, or any kind of religious ruler, contradicting the infinite creation of the prevailing Spirit. Where is the man of sense who with conscience would or could say that God does not execrate Moses, Alexander, Napoleon, and all generals who had unjustly waged war against innocent nations ? You say that man is the only being who has an immortal soul ; if so, who taught to man to imitate the lions and tigers of the forest? When the Roman people, during the times of their greatest distress, created dictators, those consuls would have lost their head, had they kept such power more than six months. Here Lincoln, having assumed the power of Moses, Alexander, or Napoleon, he robbed and murdered millions of citizens with impunity. Such an injustice had always happened, and will always, when the people permit the tyrant to be unjust. The civil laws send Tweed to the penitentiary as well as the father who robs to feed his children ; but the despot, with myrmidons at his command, has reverends who pray for him, scribblers praising him, and slaves elevating monuments to him. The infatuation of our good people is so great, that Mrs. Lincoln, with impunity, robbed all the furniture of the White House.

That the Democrats are not all angels, we repeat here again. Yes, the so-called Union or War Democrats have been slaves to the Republicans. I can prove 'it by what they did and acted on me during these last fifteen years. At the first days of Lincoln's sway, I was fully nominated, and fully elected, superintendent of the Linden schools by the Democratic party. Before the war, I had never wished to meddle myself in politics. In time of such a war, I thought it was my duty to defend my adopted country, and that of my children. But I said to my party: "You may vote for me if you think me fit for the office, but I would not offend the people by asking one single vote in my favor." The chief individuals of my party did not like me, because I blamed them for having, at that time, called themselves *Union Democrats*, an expression of sympathy toward the Whigs or Republicans. As we had, in Linden, a law for which the superintendent of the schools was obliged to have two Democrats as securities, they whispered secretly to each other, with the crafty purpose to refuse me their securities. With such a subterfuge, the Union Democrats gave my lawful office to a Republican, a certain Mr. Windsor, who was base enough to take it, and pocketed the money without doing the beneficial duty, as I intended to do myself, with honesty and capacity to the pupils.

During the time of Lincoln's terror, I gave many articles to Democratic editors. Some of them used, in part, my logic against the radicals ; but they refused to print my articles as I gave to them, fearing to have their business burned by the Whigs, or shot like dogs. Their modifications, instead of my naked truths, never pleased me. In politics, unless the truth be said without fear, it can do no good.

During the time in which General Garibaldi was invited to come to fight the confederates, I wrote to him not to come, if he wished not to lose his good reputation. As he did not answer me, I do not know yet, if the hero of my dear, native country received my letter. Mr. Ben. Wood honored me by publishing that letter in his newspaper.

Mr. M. Pomeroy did publish some of my articles, but he would not publish my best, which I thought would have done some good, and I gave him many articles. In him, I did not find the Democrat I expected. My last letter to him was written with this reproach: " You are not the Democrat whom our country is wanting, Mr. Pomeroy. The Tories, or Whigs, are the *rebels*, not the Democrats of the South, as you call them. Could I believe them rebels to our freedom, I would fight, rather than defend them, as I do." However, I had not been chained, nor killed in Fort Lafayette, as many noble citizens did suffer the death of shot dogs.

I do not doubt many patriots in the free States must have suffered in seeing such mean tyrants breaking this blessed Constitution ; but I can say that I had not met here a Democrat on whom I could rely. I wrote a letter to Mr. Charles Dana, saying that the Americans should be thankful to him for what he has done lately, by unmasking so many *honorable* thieves ; but that he could not save his country, unless he would protest against the Republicans, and confess, that our calamities were originated by the Whigs, his party. As I was inclined to believe him an innocent victim of Mr. Greeley, I asked of him the favor of wishing to publish my articles in the *Sun*, or, at least, if he were not disposed to protest against his party, to permit me to write without any trammels whatever, and that, as my object is to write the truth, I invited him, or the best political writers, to write against me and my historical facts. Mr. Dana replied politely to me, that my articles could do no good. Such honest Republicans as Mr. Dana or Mr. William C. Bryant who, even now in 1875, can not deny the evident injury done by their party, they would not say that their party did ruin this country. Only an Aristides, and such like few great men of the antiquity, would acknowledge their ignorant, innocent fault in order to save their country. The guilty authors of this civil war, by dint of having accused the confederates so long a time unjustly, now they believe their infernal falsehood to be a heavenly truth. Pull a nail from the brain of man ; it will remain the rust and the mark ! They are so blind in their own error, for which they say, That such a confession would now render useless the works of millions of victims, and injure the Union. The Republicans who have sense enough can not deny, that we have anarchy instead of union or peace ; but they have not sufficient patriotism as an Aristides, who would willingly sacrifice his personality to save his country. The Grecian patriot, obedient to the law of his country, was happy in his ostracism. Such a sound mind in America would never have united with a Lincoln to assassinate the immortal Jefferson Davis. I suppose now many Republicans must be repented for having done the criminal deeds against the Southern martyrs ; but the rogues and ruffians still in power, unless they confess and repent publicly of such war, they can not obtain the pardon of God. When Greeley and Grant were candidates for the presidency, I would have felt ashamed, had I voted for the criminal Grant, or for the editor of the *Tribune*, who advised his party to keep the Democrats *in terrorem.* The dust of Greeley's party should not be permitted to rise up to our nostrils any longer. The stink would create so many Ulysses Grants as the grasshoppers which last year plagued some of our States.

I wrote a long letter to Mr. Frank Leslie for the same object, to demonstrate in his magazine to the people, that, unless the Democrats of the North would cease from helping the Republicans, in keeping the South slaves to their black slaves, and to keep away from those States the bayonets of Grant and usurping governors ; the North would always be robbed by thieves in Congress, and mean-President. Mr. Leslie gave my letter back to his secretary, who remitted it to me without one word of polite acknowledgment. I told to the same secretary, if I could see Mr. Leslie? As the literary man was passing us, going into his cabinet, his secretary said to him, that I wished an answer to my letter, and I tendered it again to him. In putting his eyes on it, and recollecting, I suppose, the subject of it, with the greatest inurbanity, the editor turned his back to me, entered his cabinet, and shut the door to my face. I was a stranger to him, as he was a stranger to me.

I suppose his gratuitous insult must have been originated from the cloudy thundering sky which Mr. Leslie must have felt on that day, March 2d, 1873. Indeed, my Democracy must have intimated to him, the glorious election of the 3d of November, 1874, twenty months after his urbanity to me. If politeness is the principal ornament of literature, Mr. F. Leslie can not be considered a learned man, even had my letter intimated to him that his aristocracy must have an end in America.

During those infernal times of war, I was looking in every corner of New-York to find an editor who would publish the truth against the aristocratic devils, greedy of the property of the Southerners. I found only few ones who would have been pleased to publish my articles ; but they were afraid to be burned alive. However, even the most radical Black Republican editors respected my patriotic feeling. They, excepting Mr. Frank Leslie, had been all polite to me. Although I did not meet in the North a soul wishing to sympathize with me in public, at that time, I learned that, even here, the number of Democrats must have been superior to that of Whigs ; and the last 3d of November, 1874, proved it, or, at least, our calamities rendered the people wiser. If the Americans will stick to their noble fathers of one hundred years ago, these calamities of our generation will teach us wise lessons for the Republics to come, provided a new Tacitus would write these annals. But 1 would never cease from inculcating the instruction of professors, delivering public lectures of self-governments, and banishing for ever all intolerant religions, preaching, and defaming sciences and fine arts. Historical theatres are the best schools of morals and social instruction, when they will be well conducted.

This civil war is nothing else but the consequence of the revolution of one hundred years ago, against the British mother country, originated when the tea was thrown into the sea waters of Boston to free the country from this hateful tariff. Afterward that Tory party changed themselves into Whigs, Natives, Nonothings, Radicals, and at last the so-called Republicans, the mortal enemies of the Democrats, the patriots of the North and South. John Adams, the second president, was a Tory ; and his descendants, who call themselves now Republicans, are nothing else but the same Tories of one hundred years ago, the foes of George Washington. These Tories tell now nothing else but falsehoods. The so-called Republicans waged war against the confederates for no other purpose but to destroy the Constitution. Greeley, Lincoln, and stinking party lied when they said, *that their emancipation was a measure of war.* Mr. Alexander H. Stephens was mistaken in saying, *That this is a war of States.* It is a civil war. Had they not the confederate, the traitor Whigs in their own houses? Sherman and the devil conquered them on account of such traitors. The stinking party has now the impudence to say, that, were Lincoln living, the Southerners would not be kept under Grant's bayonets. Are they not the officers of the government, with the politics of Grant, and Republican Congress, robbing, proceeding, and acting with the same criminal, despotical war of Lincoln? Had not Lincoln been a Whig all his life? Have they not changed the epithet *patriotic* into *loyal?* The Railsplitter knew very well that a loyalist is a subject, adhering to his sovereign. Had he not usurped the dictatorship without our votes? Were they not the Whigs, the Tories, who fought against the fathers of this Constitution? Have they not already broken our Constitution? Were they not the foes of Andrew Jackson, the president-patriot, who unmasked the bank robbers? The Whigs, are they not tariff-men and high-taxes men? Henry Clay, was he not a gambler, and the orator of the Custom-House? Why? With their infernal Union have they not centralized the independent States?

When before the war they found that the emigrants were honest Democrats, they acted their best to prevent them from becoming citizens. The scoundrels had the impudence to say, that foreigners did not know what liberty is. Now, they have made voters and legislators out of black slaves, for no other purpose but to get their votes in order to defeat the Democrats, had they not chained, murdered, and tortured patriots? Lincoln's party, cruel and barbarous as the intolerant Jesuits of the darkest ages, ordered loafers to shoot our best citizens in Fort Lafayette!

If Grant can not succeed to murder the American liberty, it is because a jackass, on two feet, can not be a Cæsar. The Roman general was, in the art of war, greater than Alexander : he was so brave that his name is the standard of bravery, without a cigar in his mouth : he was one of the best writers of his age : he was generous, and as eloquent as Cicero. Although Lincoln was a man, by far, not to be compared with Cæsar, had he not been shot, our present Americans would have suffered him to be a crowned despot ! But, if Grant will do the same, the world will brand us: *The last of Nations!* In 1875 we have, unfortunately, many Americans who would thus ruin their country like Lincoln and Grant. Were this not an awful truth, Grant could not live now; or, at least, the Americans would have hung him long ago.

Self or Democratic government is the best for mankind to live on this planet. When telegraphs and rapid traveling will unite

all nations with justice, free commerce, tolerance of creeds, and
without national prejudices, posterity will pity and wonder, in
reading the ridiculous, useless, mad slaughters, as we do yet, to
get a supremacy which educated men hate, and cause slave to
fear. Is it not better to be loved than to live the life of the
tyrant, and be cursed even after death ?

One hundred years ago, the tariff was the cause of war in this
country. The tariff, taxes, and hateful impositions which now,
these thieves, keep us in suffering poverty, are more than we can
endure. We are still such blinded fools that, in preparing the
celebration of a centennial liberty, we do nothing but to demonstrate to the world our stupidity ! We are going to dance by
the sound of our chains and death-like music ! Can we call this
the land of the free ? It is only free for U. Grant !

Tariffs and such taxes were and are the inventions of tyrants.
When self-government will be understood, the rich will be more
happy than he had ever been : society would not grieve, nor
will see misery. The blessed political economy, as it should be,
has not yet been understood. Fifteen years ago I said here, in
the Northern States : The calamities you are going to perpetrate
into the Southerners will turn back to us. *Do not to others that
which you wish not to be done to you.* The property robbed from
the South rendered the North still poorer than it was before the
war ! The Northern States have never suffered so much as they do
now; but the few, fatten rogues, if they will not suffer before their
death, God will do justice in heaven. Taxes on furniture, taxes
on frontiers, taxes on drinks, taxes on salt, taxes on bread, taxes
on houses, taxes on our death. . . If they could, the rogues would
tax the water we drink and the air we breathe. With our money
and labor they fatten their spies, like the freedmen of Claudius
and all those Roman monsters, the horror of the antiquity. The
spies of such Custom-houses look into our trunks, boots, houses.
They mortgaged our land and bodies. This American and dis-
honorable Congress fatten speculators, buying goods and lands.
These speculators, now called millionaires, rise their prices,
keeping fathers of families in want, and force men, employed by
them, to vote for their friends, the Republicans, and for themselves. Behold our liberty !

Had George Washington thought that, after his death, these
very Tories, who gave him so much trouble, would have broken
the Constitution before one hundred years, he would not have
permitted to be elected himself as President a second term.
Had Grant any patriotism, he should have immediately said to
the slaves, wishing him to be President for a third term : My
country is dearer to me than a royal crown. The imitator of
Napoleon the Third pockets the double fee, robs the public
treasury with the stinking Congress, and sends bandits into

those assassinated States to crown himself with bayonets. This criminal, called President, whose best knowledge is to smoke cigars ; who sent poor soldiers to the mouths of cannons, placing himself where no shot could touch him ; who with anarchy expects to crown himself a chief despot ; keeping under bayonets the living robbed martyrs, such a beast, is called *Excellency!*

On January 10th, 1875, Senator Schurz blamed Grant without blaming Lincoln. He said : *The American people hold as sacred, as the life-element of their Republican freedom, the right to govern and administer their local affairs independently.* Mr. Schurz should have known that, had not Lincoln been shot, he would be now crowned a despot long ago. Had not Lincoln usurped the dictatorship without our consent ? Sheridan, Belknap, Grant, and the Devil, they would not have dreamed to ruin the country without such an infernal instruction of the railsplitter.

The letters of P. H. Sheridan on January 4th and 5th, 1875, are letters of a mean slave and traitor to his country. He is no better than Tigellinus, the ruffian of Nero during the middle century of Christ in Rome ; and, what is still more disgusting, such a beast assumed the ermine of justice. The *Harper's Bazar* had the impudence to call the dirty traitors, *the bulwark of American liberty!* Were the traitors hung by the insulted people, the *beautiful editors*, without hesitation, would give a kick to their corpses, like the jackass of the fable. The Harpers are enraged against the honest Democrats : their political trash of despotism, and praising their Excellency, brings nausea into the stomach of ladies and gentlemen, who understand what liberty is. Their sauciness, boast, and arrogance demonstrate what kind of booksellers they are. The disgusting pirates who robbed, and rob the lawful rights of American and English literature, are cursed by English and American writers.

Many pigmies, I know, will fulminate the anathema against me ; but I know also that the historians must look to heaven. Union is wisdom. Ignorance is discord. Union is liberty. Discord is this war and this infernal peace of Grant. This anarchy is fomented for no other purpose but to suppress the *habeas corpus* with bayonets and hinder the best Democrats to vote. Mankind had not, is not, nor will be united by the sword. This present confusion of thieves, is it not an anarchy ? Alexander the Great, or the cannons of Napoleon the First, had ever united men ? The mind of man is more free than electric. You can confine the fluid into a bottle : but chain the brave man in your despotical dungeon ; he curses you, even when you, monsters, roast him to death ! Our noble race can only be united by kindness, love, and justice ; and the true religion of God, which is heaven, not your hell.

I am acquainted with half a dozen of languages : the Italian is the best I know of them. Benevolent readers, I say this thing to you, with the object that you must not expect from me the language of an Addison, Pope, nor Byron. I can say, however, that these pages breathe such an honesty, to force blushes of shame on the cheeks of Radicals, if they have not lost their senses. I permit any fool to take up his dirty pen, lie against me, or against my political logic of self-government.

I attempted to publish this Drama, even under the terror of Lincoln. Of course no publisher, printer, nor bookseller wished to have any thing to do with this work, during that time ; and my madness against Satan prevented me from seeing, that I was putting my head into the lion's mouth. I could not see that, and even, had this work been published in that time, it could not save the country, for the reason that the whole Northern States, against the South, had culminated to blind madness.

Had I been Governor Horatio Seymour, I would have done my best to prevent General Dix to break the Constitution, in usurping the governorship of New-York. I would have prevented those free citizens to become soldiers of such tyrants. Had the lawful governor.armed them against the despotical bayonets of the unlawful dictator, he could save the country from these shameful calamities.

Honest, suffering citizens of America, if the last one hundred years of your history do not make you wiser, you can not pretend to be an intelligent nation, nor to call this, the land of the free. Since this blessed Constitution, written by your noble fathers, to the time in which Lincoln usurped the dictatorship, you passed eighty-five years in a blessing independence of a democratic government, in spite of Henry Clay and stinking party. If these last fifteen years of robberies, murders, and incendiaries have not cured you from your infatuation, and you will still vote for your tyrants, you must expect to suffer a greater slavery for yourselves than the bondage of the black Africans. Read the annals and history of Tacitus, and you can see the calamities in which these monsters are preparing for you and unborn Americans. Can we expect the promised Eden on earth, when our indolence permits devils to rob our rights and independence ?

It is now 1875 years since the voice of Jesus echoed for peace in the Jewish temple of Jerusalem. He called the circumcised, stained with the blood of robbed nations, vipers and hypocrites. If not all, many reverends of Luther and Calvin on every Sunday exalt the morals of God's peace ; but when Abels, by millions, were murdered, martyred, robbed, and burned ; the Cains in their temples, with bloody flags, hurrah at the agonies of their brethren ! Rev. Beecher, selling lies in England, was slandering the tortured Confederates with the never-ending cant as : *mongers of negroes*, the very negroes kidnapped from the shores of Africa and sold to the belligerent, not rebellious, seceders by the father and grandfather of the same Rev. Beecher, so much praised, improperly, by the guilty Republicans, alias Whigs. Any individual denying or acknowledging himself guilty of this historical fact, if not repented, he should not be permitted to stand as a witness in a court of justice. We should not believe such men any better than we can believe Pope Borgia, or a rich learned or eloquent hypocrite of Plymouth Church. When shall we value men by their intrinsic merit, and not by their tricks? The nation, judging the citizens by the standard of any intolerant religion is a nation of monks. Were Brooklyn not a city of monks, the eloquence of a Rev. Beecher would not have defiled so many women. The citizens suspecting such men, and for fear of losing their direct interest, do not expose bravely the corrupter of society, under garments of Christianity, is a coward slave who, for not having shouted *fire* in time, left the whole city to be burned. An eloquent mortal sinner is as bad as an incendiary. Those Judas or lawyers who attempted, lately, to deprive Theodore Tilton from the benefit of civil justice for having Tilton said that he does not think Jesus to be the only begotten Son of God, are nothing better than the intolerant Spanish Torqueada, who burned alive gentlemen with that infernal Inquisition.

Beloved Americans! our best friends are those who demonstrate our faults to us, and our foes, those who flatter us. If our country might return great as it was fifteen years ago, we must thank noble citizens who, like Charles A. Dana, the editor of the *Sun*, have unmasked many Americans bad as Roman Augustus, Tiberius, Nero, or Tigellinus, the shame of yore Italy, my dear country, where I was born. Certainly, *il re Galantuomo*, in present Europe is not permitted to be as one of the above tigers without restraint of laws, in the beginning of Christianity; but we are still barbarian by permitting a king to be above the civil laws, for no other reason but for being the son of another king. King Emmanuel must think himself above the sons of Adam. He must think himself superior to the woman he loves. His morganatic marriage proves his false pride. If arrogance degrades a man, to expose ourselves to be insulted by the arrogant is a submission not to be praised by the wise. When Princess Clotilde Buonaparte came to New-York, I sent to her an ode on Italy. I did it because she had the reputation as being an angel of modesty; besides, I thought her to be a grateful woman, even to such an obscure man as I am. Had I been a Jesuit, as I heard afterward, she would have invited me to see her in this strange country. *Il Cavaliere Montiglio*, ex-president of the Chamber of the King, her great-grandfather, and his brother from Casale, having been my dear friends, I was very anxious to hear from her of their honorable and beloved families. At my age, I should have known what kind of stuff is a princess, and thus not expose myself to her royal, silent sliding.

With *the wishing to be a prince,* I do not blame myself. Of Mr. Frank Leslie I had a hearty laugh, which did me some benefit, in seeing a Republican buffoon playing the clownish prince. My dear father and mother, the princess and the republican, will be buried like the rest of us all. The monument of A. Lincoln, will also crumble to dust ! Benevolence toward the whole human family is immortal.

ARGUMENT.

Col. Anthony and Mrs. Charlotte Rovellini, both from Massachusetts, had a son and a daughter. Charles, the first-born, and the protagonist of this Drama, was betrothed to Miss Virginia Holmes, a rich young lady of the South.

During the dictatorship of Abraham Lincoln, the Rovellini family lived in New-York. Mother, son, and daughter were patriotic worshipers of their sacred Constitution of the United States of North America. The father was a Tory, sympathizing with American aristocracy, or falsely called Republicans.

Family dissension is the subject of Act I. ; the despotic draft Act II. ; Act III., the desertion of Charles ; a martial trial, Act IV. ; and Act V., the death of Charles and Virginia, with reconciliation in heaven.

PERSONS.

Anthony,
Charles, ⎫
Charlotte, ⎬ Rovellini.
Alaska,   ⎭

Virginia Holmes.
Alphonso Spangler.
Judge.
Reverend Thompson.
People.
Jury of Twelve Soldiers.
Generals.
Captains.
Officers.
Soldiers.

Scene.—*House of Colonel Anthony Rovellini in New-York;
afterward the Camp of the Army of Potomac in America.*

ACT I.

SCENE I.

ANTHONY, CHARLES.

ANTHONY.

Your love for Holmes Virginia blinds you now ;
This poor, unhappy country do protect.

CHARLES.

I fear that you feel not our country's love.

ANTHONY.

Do, be my son.

CHARLES.

          My duty does not fail ;
But that of citizen I feel likewise.
I did, I do, and still I will pray Heaven,
That you may feel the citizen's high duty.
Oh ! do, I pray, give up your party, father.

ANTHONY.

Lincoln, the elected President, should rule
The government. You should not hinder, Charles,
The administration. Wicked times are these.

CHARLES.

The South is not rebellious. I was not
Yet born when you were Tories, though called Whigs :
You were rebellious to the country's laws.
Was not this President against the Union ?
It was his wish to disunite the States :
Read, read our history, and then be just.
Now, with the Union painted on the flag,
Brothers 'gainst brothers, he with jokes excites ;
Fathers against the sons. He wished to reign,

And reigns. With taxes, citizens he robs ;
Infamous votes he buys ; in prisons locks,
Unlawfully, Americans born free.

ANTHONY.

But is not terror in these times required ?

CHARLES.

After your base insults, the South secedes :
The South does not wage war on these free States.
Upon their slaves you have no right. The tyrant
Has bought the Senate. Now, with him, against
The Constitution, they conspire. They wage,
On brothers, brutal war : the North is kept
In bonds. Are we not slaves to them ?

ANTHONY.

You traitor . . .

CHARLES.

Of this, our land, the traitors are the Whigs.

ANTHONY.

You should be sent to jail.

CHARLES.

Do not delay.
Have we no martial laws ? You should denounce
Your son in this fanantic, servile war.
Missouri, Orleans, Maryland, all States
The tyrants have reduced in ruin. Born
Beggars, and basely proud, in brutal power
They glory. Southern whites they put in bonds,
And into thieves they change the freedmen blacks.
From the first President until these days,
The name Republican was false in you :
Of the best citizens, you are the foes.
With changing times you ever change your name.
Of this premeditated war you wished
Made Henry Clay your chief, when he was living.
Three candidates the Democrats, against
Your Lincoln, had. Our votes divided thus,
Against the people's will you did prevail.
It should have been a mourning day, the day
In which your Lincoln entered Washington.
You, with the craft to centralize the States,

Silver and gold from rich and poor extorted.
Not all the Democrats, as Whigs, are crafty ;
By your corrupted press deceived, to your
Speakers they went to listen to your self
Boasting. The great Roman, the censor Cato,
Permitted would he have such boasting Whigs
To speak such language as deserves the lash ?
Are we not slaves already ? But your son
Would rather die the death of a free man.

ANTHONY.

Call you a country free, where slaves by millions
Are kept in bonds ?

CHARLES.

Our greatest evil's this !
But your own father, did he not buy slaves ?
And did he not sell them ? The just forefather
Of dear Virginia had he not bought slaves,
Slaves from your father ? Are not we now rich ?
This wealth, which our ancestors gave to us,
Was it not gained by interchange of slaves,
Robbed from the shores of Africa ? Did not
Bostonians bring negroes to the North ?
Still greater is our infamy ! The South
Bought them : you kidnapped them and sold for gold.
What right have you to free the negroes, whom
You, to your brothers of the South, did sell ?
With sword in hand, you cut their masters' throats,
And burn their houses !

ANTHONY.

We no more have slaves ;
The South should have emancipated them,
As we did.

CHARLES.

Irish, Dutch from Europe came
Into these States to bless with work, and free
This country from such evil. Emancipation,
Time, patience, and instruction will free them,
As we have done, as well as Greece and Rome.
Slaves to the South belong, and to the North
Counsels of peaceful Gospel. Lincoln has
No right to free the slaves. Do they belong
To him ? Our great audacity the South
Has not, nor wish to rule these States of ours.
Do not unite yourself to such base tyrants.

ANTHONY.

The Southerners are tyrants to their slaves.

CHARLES.

Your very crimes in your own neighbor spurn.
To your party you wish to bind me slave !
When your thoughts were unknown to me, most dear
To me you were. Are you now equal to
Your master, who himself did place above
The law ? Unjust to soldiers you may be ;
Lincoln may be to you unjust. Your master,
Already, is the President. You know
Not, or, at least, you do not wish to know
The hateful curse of your perverted party.
Three years ago, with sacred laws we were
Independent. What right have you, without
Just cause, without the judgment of the court,
To send me now to your bastiles to rot ?
By passion, rancor, now to infernal counsels
Moved are you. Pray not to repent too late !
To thoughtless men, revenge is mighty sweet.
Yes, for your valiant deed, to you was given
Of warlike glory world-wide fame ; but, father,
The very generals who tyrants are
To citizens, are they not Lincoln's slaves ?
With degradation their lost battles were
Requited. If McClellan were recalled
To the command of the army, he'd receive
The tyrant's order still. Each public place
Of this poor land is held by mean white slaves.
The Latin Romans are not known by us :
This age feels not the noble, generous thought
Of liberty. The General and jailer
Of Baltimore holds negroes in the jails,
Because they wish not fight against their masters ;
They were not slaves to them, but grateful servants.

SCENE II.

CHARLOTTE, and the Same.

CHARLOTTE.

My son, dear husband, cease. You wound my heart
With your dispute.

ANTHONY.

To government is Charles
The greatest foe, as well to me.

CHARLES.

The foe
I am of tyrants, and the friend of our
Free laws and Constitution.   Citizens
We have who may be worthy of Jefferson,
Monroe. and Washington ; but now such men
We can not find, unless we look among
The Democrats.   The Union of the Whigs
Is union of perdition.   Can you hope
With those whose cities you have burned, to join
In brothers' love ?   Blood, crimes the most robust
Stare at your face in every place you go :
Rapes, desolation, famine censure you !
And still you do not blush?   What right have you
Upon the very slaves, whom you did sell?
Your base pretext to free the slaves is false.
You, many times have changed your party's name :
Republicans, Know-nothings, Natives, Whigs
Are nothing else but Tories.   On my party
With Henry Clay you did wage war : you now
Feel not ashamed to praise the immortal Jackson,
Whom you abused in life and his own party.
You were the foes of Andrew Jackson ; but
Now, him who sleeps the sleep of death, you praise,
Praise falsely him, whom you've misused.   Have you
Forgot the threats, insults, in his lifetime,
You gave to him, through Henry Clay, you Whigs?
Had you not, with the tariff, robbed the South?
And now, with money robbed from us, and taxes
Upon the air we breathe, you murder those
Who leave you free, and wish be left alone.
Silver and gold, your gods, the tariff, bank,
And aristocracy have always kept
You, from the sacred freedom, dear to me.
And now that you are rich, you buy the titles
Of lords, marquis, princes, kings.   Of our sons
The shame and horror we shall be, when these
Calamities described will be by true
Historians.   The newspapers of the North,
Excepting only few, are sold to Whigs :
In Lafayette, the Democrats are locked
For having branded bloody deeds of shame.
In servile silence you force us to weep.
Missouri, Texas, Maryland, Kentucky
Are under tyrant laws as Northern States.
The infernal monster, Jennison, commands

The slaves to march upon their dying masters :
Upon the masters, tears of grateful servants
Pour, mingled with their blood. This is the time
To weep, America ! If you do not,
When will you weep ? Behold Lucretias there ;
American Camillas hanging from
The branches of the trees. Those flames which reach
The clouds, adding to night horror and shame,
Unveil to Christians their infernal deeds.
Women and girls in bed, an hour ago,
They dreamed the death of their beloved ones :
Almost naked, disheveled, now they run
To save their lives and honor. Hear the yells,
The laughs of soldiers ! Daughters of our land
Are dragged by lustful loafers to the woods !
A black cloud falls before my sight ! My mind
With madness asks revenge. One Cheever, many
Ministers of the Devil, war they preach
In churches consecrated to blest peace.
Unchristian pride erected your rich temples,
While Christian poor you leave to die by want :
Unchristian pride fats Beecher, selling lies
In Europe, while you starve, sack, murder, burn,
Ravish the South, defending dying children.
Apostles of poor Christ were nobly poor ;
On tops of huts they preached divine precepts,
Forbearance, peace, and love toward the neighbor ;
You, reformed men and women, without shame
Applaud now human slaughter ! Bloody flags
Upon the steeples of unchristian pride
Inculcate terror into Christian minds :
You would nail Jesus on the cross again.

CHARLOTTE.

What answer, Colonel, must to him return ?

ANTHONY.

Charles is a traitor, rebel. . . .

CHARLOTTE.

          Traitress, rebel
With Charles, therefore, am I. Deceived we all,
By this administration, are. Myself
A shield will be to Charles. Against the laws
Of liberty he is drafted. Wishes not,

Nor he can, 'gainst the brothers of Virginia,
Her friends, and father, fight: betrothed to her
Is Charles. You hope in vain to change his heart.

CHARLES.

Were not Virginia dear to me, my mother,
My country ever must be dear to me.
Deceived were all the volunteers by this
President: mocked we should not be by him.
Against the people's will, he can not be
Executive of our laws, nor without
Plural consent: he broke our sacred laws,
By placing senators in Congress, not
'Elected by free votes.

ANTHONY.

In times of war,
Dictators are required.

CHARLES.

No; we would not
Wage war against the South. If not himself,
Who did elect dictator him? Rebellious
Is Lincoln; an usurper of our rights.
Such dictators the Romans put to death.

ANTHONY.

In order to subdue ferocious minds,
The martial terror should be now enforced:
The death of traitor you deserve. Denounce
You now I must; you force me.

CHARLOTTE.

When your menace
Will have effect, I mother am to Charles;
Your sword must pass this breast. With such a son,
This country might not yet be lost.

ANTHONY.

You both
I, now abhor.

CHARLES.

Abhor I can not you.
Father, I pity you. Your mortal foe
I should be, were I not your son.

CHARLOTTE.

To free
From tyrants Rome, Brutus condemned his sons.
For these base tyrants, shame of this fair land,
You wish to sacrifice your son ; wage war
Against the father, brothers of Virginia,
Who've been insulted these last forty years !
To Democrats the Whigs are mortal foes :
Your Union is a trick. You slaughter those
Who do not wish to help your party. Coachmen
Do we not see in livery ? Are those
The signs of a republic?

CHARLES.

Reason, mother,
Does not avail with tyrants. Force with force
Should be repulsed, or die. . . .

ANTHONY.

No more I wish
Taunting insults to hear. Between us peace
Will never be. Were it my party's duty
To plunge my sword into your heart ; if fate
Claims me to die by parricidal hand,
Under your sword, I brand myself a coward,
Should I retreat from that horrible death.

ACT II.

SCENE I.

ANTHONY.

Were, as the Romans, great my fellow-men,
I would encourage Charles in lofty thoughts.
The lives of great Plutarch made him my foe :
As Cato, Brutus ; Charles feels now the pang.
His country's love will not lead him to fortune.
Were I, like him, exciting men to rise
To thoughts, now lost, of buried great-grandfathers,
As mad as Charles I should be. Them I see
Trembling before the martial laws. 'Gaiust me,
Against his interest he's all intent.
Respect I can not have for men who look
To their own wealth, without the love of country !. . .
But, change can I the spirit of the times ?
Such virtue I have not, wish not. If I
So great a man could be, too well I see
That I might fall a victim, as my son.
Oh ! to be praised I long in war, among
My fellow-beings. In the free States, I see
That many love the glory of Napoleon.
Immortal Washingtons or Cincinnatus
Not in the North are found, but in the South,
Where 'gainst invasion they defend their homes.
I do the South respect as much as Charles ;
But my self-love now forces me to follow
The wicked North for better life and wealth.
Were it the surest, liberty would I
Select than monarchy. Brutus nor Cato
Can now give us the virtue we have not.
In ostentation, princely life, and shows,
Emp'rors, ministers, kings, we mimic now :
To Russian subjects balls, luxurious parties
We give. The President is now united
With the same Czar who slaughters noble Poles
Fighting so bravely for their household gods.

SCENE II.

ALPHONSO, *and the Same.*

ANTHONY.

General, what news?

ALPHONSO.

The men now go to draft.
I think the Yorkers are disposed to rise :
Traitors we have with us, friends to the South.

ANTHONY.

The mobs without a captain are like oxen ;
To slaughter with a stick, a boy may drive them.

ALPHONSO.

Robespierre ruled with terror a French crowd
Of noblemen in Paris, during times
Given to court's corruption, vice, and lust.
Americans are not like French : are like
Romans in those ferocious times of freedom,
So hard to be conducted by patricians.
Americans have not forgot their freedom
Which, from their minds, with skill, we must blot out.

ANTHONY.

They dare not face the soldiers drilled.

ALPHONSO.

We can not
Place confidence in legions yet untried.

ANTHONY.

More than two years the volunteers are drilled :
All the gen'rals and colonels are now sworn ;
McClellan was dismissed for not concurring
With our emancipation, loyal league,
And President. The soldiers in this war
Are trained to sack : the children's, women's tears
Caused them to laugh. Ministers of the gospel
Have in the churches preached, that traitor South
Are cursed by God now to destruction, having
Against the government rebelled. The negroes
Whom we have freed, force nations to proclaim
Us champions of humanity. Without

Impediment, the mob will be conducted
Into bad life : delights bad men the blood :
Thirsty for blood, like drunkards, the art of war
Leads them from blood to blood.   Often I've heard
My soldiers wish to plunge a bayonet
Into their sister's, brother's, father's heart,
For having blamed this war we wage to South.
Thousands of volunteers enrolled we have
For a protracted war.

ALPHONSO.

It is the war
Against the Democrats which us sustains.
They think that we wage war upon the South,
To force them into Union : fools, and worse !
If Democrats and South could once unite,
No more Whig presidents could rule this country
For time to come.   They think we fight for Union,
Free government : our party we defend,
And not this Constitution, which was, is,
Will be the foe to Whigs.   The fools united
With us ; with us they slaughter their party,
And of the South, their friends, whom we call *rebels*.
Our cause they favor with the war, although
They do not fear to show themselves the foes
Of Whigs in power now ; they are the tools
Of our revenge.   Perhaps we have with us
The greater part of their own party here,
In the North : of the South, we have with us
The Whigs in greater part, and Puritans ;
But if we do not kill the rebels all,
Our party fore'er lost would be.   The South,
The Constitution, and free laws must be
Pulled down, and with them all the citizens
Of Democratic party.   Union, war
Democrats with us will go, when power
We have with us, and soldiers : these prefer
To have for President and leaders, men
Fond of the sword, and not the men of peace.

ANTHONY.

The Northern Democrats are now divided :
The Democrats for war, against their will,
Help us ; and those for peace are curbed, laughed at.

ALPHONSO.

We hold two-thirds of Whigs in Congress now :
Against peace Democrats they have passed laws.

In other times, the many formed the laws.
But now they do not dare to speak 'gainst us.
We now have martial laws ; many are held
As rebels, traitors. We have with us many
Soldiers, whose business, interest, is war. . . .
Alaska comes in haste.

SCENE III.

ALASKA, *and the Same.*

ANTHONY.

Pray, daughter, speak.

ALASKA.

The city's in commotion. Wrapt in flames
Is now the drafting house.

ALPHONSO.

Do, Colonel, come ;

Must not delay.

ANTHONY.

At your command am I.

SCENE IV.

ALASKA.

Loyal to whom ? We loyal should not be
To those who have usurped our sacred freedom.
I can not live much longer in these States :
We can not act nor speak against the tyrants ;
The truth is now opproprious to them ;
This war, which should shame them, has rendered them
Most odious to the citizens : with terror,
Prisons, and death, their cowardice they shield.
My dear Virginia, your words move my heart !
These words of General Lee move me to tears ![1]
" Our property they rob ; the cities burn;
  Unarmed sisters, the mothers, children ask
  Of you their safety, liberty. Their faith

[1] *Reads.*

Is placed in you. Let us remember our
Duty. To die upon the battle-field
For such high cause of God is now man's pride.
The bloody fields for vengeance cry aloud ;
They, Justice, Country, God demand of us."

SCENE V.

CHARLOTTE, *and the Same.*

ALASKA.

Has Charles not yet arrived ?

CHARLOTTE.

Not yet, my daughter.

ALASKA.

I fear his courage may lead him to death. [1]

CHARLOTTE.

Alaska, I feel unhappy.

ALASKA.

For what cause ?

CHARLOTTE.

An honest citizen is Charles ; but father,
Like Lincoln, is a Whig.

ALASKA.

The Whigs are traitors.

CHARLOTTE.

Your father is our foe.

ALASKA.

I feel it also.
Our home is in dissent. My father loves
You not, as he did once.

[1] *Noise of the people in the streets, with fire-companies running,
and crying, "Fire !"*

CHARLOTTE.

          In their own hands
They hold the country, and will make us slaves.
That noble Andrew Jackson was insulted
During his life, when they robbed us with banks
Of paper money. Now they rob still more,
And praise him in the grave. Republicans
Call now themselves, and Unionists, not Whigs,
Not Natives, with intent still more to plunder.

ALASKA.

Lincoln is not so crafty as he boasts ;
He has confessed to have e'er had in view
The freedom of the slaves.

CHARLOTTE.

          Therefore the South
Did right to separate. His proclamation,
As a war measure, plainly contradicts
His former saying : it condemns his act.
If freedom of the slaves was his intent,
The day on which they named him President,
His proclamation should not be of war
A lying measure. Such an act would now
Be naught, but crime added to former crime.
Is not the language this of wolf to lamb ?

SCENE VI.

CHARLES, *and the Same.*

ALASKA.

O Charles ! at last you come.

CHARLES.

          They wish to burn
The city. Many houses are in flames.
All negroes they can find or meet they kill :
The blacks' asylum is reduced to ashes.
They don't permit the firemen to quench
The flames. With danger of my own, I saved
A negro's life. I heard them madly saying,
They wish to burn this house. I come in haste....
Oh ! Heaven be praised ! I see they have spared us.

ALASKA.

We heard a din of mob ; but we have not
Heard such a threat. It is all quiet now.

CHARLES.

With their emancipation they have turned
The North in their own favor : still had they
Proclaimed the same, two years before, not one
From Democrats would have sustained such act,
Which should be punished by the Constitution.
They can not pass such law without consent
Of Southern citizens and of the North.

CHARLOTTE.

Nor would our fathers suffer Christian preachers
Exciting armies to unchristian war.
We were the first who gave the slave the freedom :
The South, without compulsion, would have done
The same. The North with good example, not
With sword in hand, should teach their brother States.
How can they teach with good example, while
They have committed crimes in church and court?
Their sermons and their speeches to the public,
Bigot but horror, shame in this republic.
With beams in their own eyes, they see the mote
In their best neighbors. Demons are in hood,
As well in fashion. France is not alone
The nation, who gave birth to sans culottes :
But if the ragged· wretches 'gainst the kings
And aristocracy have been the shame
Of humankind, what should we say to monsters
Who trample under foot our Constitution,
Our laws, and Roman right in this great country ?

CHARLES.

The thieves are not ashamed to pray in church.
Not for the Union ; to the extermination
Of the best whites, they wage this war, to free
The negroes, and become themselves the masters.
The soldiers are more slaves to them than negroes :
With bayonets they keep us in contempt ;
They laugh at us with war and their Disunion.

ALASKA.

If Guatimala, Yucatan, if Cuba,
Or Canada have been disposed to form
With us a liberal compact, when we
Were free and happy, never will they now.

CHARLES.

The doctrine of Monroe is gone forever :
With us the nations will no more unite ;
This brutal, servile war has placed on guard
All nations : lost have we respect ; they would
Not trust Americans, now kept in chains,
Frightened by Whigs, without free thought, nor law.
Europe respect the South with arms in hands ;
For us, and tyrants, they now feel contempt.

CHARLOTTE.

The South for Lincoln did not vote : re-elected
Without the bayonets, he can not be.
In aristocracy they wish to change
This Constitution crafty Whigs, and false
Divines, the curse of noble men and heaven.

———

SCENE VII.]'

People, and the Same.

PEOPLE.¹

Fire ! fire ! This is the house ; it is the home '
Of an aristocrat and Black Republican.

CHARLES. ²

You should not wrong yourselves, nor act like fools !
Why you now burn the houses of your friends?
From acts so criminal you should desist.
Our cause is sacred ! This administration
To draft unwilling citizens should not.
Oh ! with the murders and the burning houses,

¹ *From the street.*
² *From the balcony at the background of the scene.*

You have already ruined your best friends,
Yourselves ! Your mad revenge against your foes,
Sadly will turn against yourselves. What shall
I say of your own friends, whom you have ruined,
And of the Blacks' asylum, in the ground?
To needy Blacks that mansion was erected,
Poorer, by far, than you ! Your acts will be
To you and Democrats a crime most black.
What good you now expect from such fool deeds ?
Oh! this, will ever be from tyrant foes
An argument against you all, and me !

PEOPLE.

We, too, condemn the thieves who burn to steal.

CHARLES.

We should unite against such crimes, my friends.
Enrolled am I like you. I swear to you
That I will never fight the Southern States.
Our friends are they, and foes to these fanatics,
Against the martial laws and all base tyrants.
Our government is not the tyrant's will.
The South secedes ; has never been rebellious.
Resistance we should use against these traitors
To constitution, government, and laws.
When in compact with us the South united,
Not to the dogs they flung away their rights,
Nor more than we have done in glorious times
Rights sacred to the States, for which they fought
With us, against the mother country. Free
With us they did unite, and free should go :
Were it not so, could this be a Republic ?
Of Black Republicans the central sway,
This continent should not admit, nor suffer.
If it were not permitted to the South
Their own free government, without control
Of Northern interest, the Polish serfs
Would be more free than Southern States. The South
They have insulted, these last forty years,
With abolition and the custom-house.
More than one Brown, the Puritans have sent
To cut their throats, and free their servant negroes.
If they would not pollute their hands, their morals,
Christianity with South, nor their chaste minds ;
Union with them is not a shameful lie?
Since Whigs pretend to be such Christian saints,

Why then unite themselves with South depraved?
A cheating word is not the Lincoln's Union?
If South leave us to do what most we please,'
Why should we not permit the same to them?
Their greatest wish is to be free from us. ·
Were we not arrogant, we should confess,
That we have been dependent of the South.
Without their great product of cotton raw,
The looms of Northern people could not work,
Nor can. Since we must need confess we stand
On equal foot of helping one another,
What right have we to make them slaves to us?
If we, with them can not govern in peace,
We can with useful commerce do still better.
The war which is now waged for lying Union
Is nothing but a party war, a party
Of many years, raised by the crafty Whigs,
For offices, and rule an honest party.
The South would live in peace, if not abused ;
They better know the Roman rights than North.
False Christians are ·the Whigs, the Puritans ;
Their *honest* Lincoln,· and his traitors, minions.
The Southern cities are reduced to ruin
By conflagrations, murders, rapes, and sacks.
With their Greek fires and shells, they wish to burn
Charleston, where women, children starve to death!
To save their wives, their mothers, and their children,
They hold in that unhappy, starving city,
The Northern soldiers, captured in the fields.
Of such defense no tiger should complain :
Still, gallant Beauregard they called a Goth,
For having non-combatants thus defended.
They say: We can not burn you there, unless
You take from rebel city Northern soldiers.
To please the hungry wolves they must turn lambs.
The saucy Lincolnites speak like mad babies.
In these bastiles, they shot most noble men,
Whose speeches charged the guards with bloody deeds,
The guards, I say, of mortal sins and crimes :
Such bloody deeds, which have no parallel,
Have they with halter punished? They rewarded them !
Against chaste husbands, and the purest wives,
Infernal deeds of lust and prostitution,
With such ferocious rage were perpetrated,
That, if not Lincoln's minions, beasts should blush.
A Northern myrmidon, who kept in chains
The husband of a lady he coveted

To prostitute, condemned the brave to die.
The wife, prostrated to the devil's feet,
Besought her husband's life.   The lustful beast
Would not consent to grant the soldier's life,
Unless she would submit to prostitution,
And pay five or six hundred dollars fine. . . .
But, when the hateful crime was perpetrated,
To 'scape the just revenge of sacred love,
He murdered still the husband in his dungeon,
And left to die with shame the outraged wife.
Behold the darlings of emancipation,
Who force you now to fight, and free the slaves,
The very blacks whom they have sold to South!
The whitened fields of human bones from heaven
Vengeance implore.   The governor may have
Magnificent, civilian virtues ; but
He was not born to lead the brave.   He should
Not have permitted Dix to govern us.
Our governor is Seymour, and not Dix.
They keep the martial laws with myrmidons.
Our blessed country, liberty they rob !
To fight the Whigs we must, or blush for shame.

PEOPLE.

May God preserve your father's house from harm,
May Heaven protect your life, which might one day
Defend us all, against these Tories, foes
To virtue, liberty, and sacred laws. [1]

[1] CHARLOTTE *and* ALASKA *prostrate themselves on their knees.*

ACT III.

SCENE I.

Camp of the Potomac with Tents.

GENERALS, OFFICERS, SOLDIERS, CHARLOTTE AND ALASKA.

CHARLOTTE.

Before us, Charles and father had arrived
In camp.

ALASKA.

I have obtained a pass, and soon
Shall see Virginia.

CHARLOTTE.

These vile usurpers
Have now arrested many noble ladies,
Defamed, insulted others in the streets.

ALASKA.

Infamous laws in Congress they have passed :
Citizens, who submit can not themselves,
They banish, confiscate their household goods
And lands.   Butler, who shed so many tears
Upon his famished prisoners of war,
Both robbed and hanged the Southern citizens,
Because to him they neither would submit
Nor own allegiance to his portly beauty.
Their brutal laws are now the stronger laws ;
They call us traitors ; us whom have betrayed !

CHARLOTTE.

These are the sons of Tories, who betrayed
The fathers of this country.   They betrayed
Our Washington ; these Whigs betray now Davis.
On the first day, when Lincoln came to power

In the White Hall, had he his guilty deed
Expressed to free the slaves, no Democrat
He could have found to break with him the law.
Who dared to speak against his bad designs,
Are locked in prison and bastiles. One million
Of buried men claim vengeance from just Heaven :
The mutilated in the streets entreat
For bread in ragged uniform ; of hunger,
Old mothers, sisters, wives, and children die :
Loafers and spies report the words and deeds
Of generous Americans, who can
Not see their country mourning, weeping, dying.
To the true Democrats is not permitted
The right of their free vote. John Brown, with death,
Had paid in Old Dominion for his crime :
With equal punishment should Lincoln pay,
Having, with proclamation, set slaves free,
Without the Congress, nor the people's votes,
Slaves, whom the guilty North sold to the South.
They have horror surpassed of Saint Domingo,
With slaughter, fire ! The history has written,
And branded in our face disgrace and crime.

ALASKA.

If Brown was properly condemned to death,
So Lincoln for his crime should be condemned :
His second crime can not wash out the first ;
A stain of blood can not be cleansed with blood
He should confess that he betrayed the South.

CHARLOTTE.

With terror, death, he keeps the nation down,
Hinders the Democrats to think, to act.
Men see a monster in the hateful tyrant,
And still against the brute to speak dare not.
The many, who are blind to virtue's deeds,
Their manly thought is to enrich themselves
Upon their conquered brothers ; and the few
Better men, who their country have at heart,
Lose all the hope of seeing again their dear
Lost liberty. There are too many base ones,
For which they can not feel the love of country.
We have here public talkers, odious editors,
Doctors and preachers, blasphemers of Christ.
Great Washington is called by them slave-monger.

ALASKA.

Oh ! General Spangler is not far from us.

SCENE II.

ALPHONSO, *and the Same.*

ALPHONSO.

Ladies, I am surprised to find you here.

CHARLOTTE.

Is in the camp my son ?

ALPHONSO.

Not distant far.

ALASKA.

Permit me, Gen'ral. . . . Mother, I must go. . . .

CHARLOTTE.

I come with you.   I must see Charles with you.

ALPHONSO.

Ladies, I'll go with you, if you desire.

CHARLOTTE.

I thank you kindly, Gen'ral, but I wish
To see my son alone.

ALPHONSO.

Do so, do so.

CHARLOTTE.

Coming to you, I see the Colonel now.

———

SCENE III.

ALPHONSO. ANTHONY.

ANTHONY.

Easily people we have led so far
From New-York.   With decided mind, a gen'ral
Can lead his men against their friends and brothers.
The drafting day was wanting martial force :

Had we been properly prepared, we could
Have saved burned homes, blood ; but though New-York
Seems calm ; although my son is in the camp,
Now here enrolled, I know too much my son
To be myself at rest.

ALPHONSO.

Yes ; very seldom
Can I see him.   In solitude, alone,
He goes about : in tears often I caught
Him in the woods.   Could you believe ?   I know
That Charles do not like us ; still, I love him.

ANTHONY.

Our foe my son is not.   The South he favors,
Because he loves Virginia, his betrothed.
Her father, mother, brothers, servants weep
In great misfortune : some are killed.   Charles can
Not hate us : generosity he has :
He does not know what hatred is : against
You, against me, he would conduct an army
Without bad feeling.   Inferior to him
I feel myself ; and still, I would not yield
To his exalted mind.   I love him much
As any father, such dear son, can love.
Th' annals of that great French Revolution,
Of liberty the foe forced me to be.
Oh ! Charles would rather die than injure me.
His mind has always been most great, sublime.
Stranger being Charles to fear, he can not hate :
His lofty mind feels now contempt, not hate.

SCENE IV. [1]

CHARLES,[2] *and the Same.*

ANTHONY.

The President is sending you the rank
Of colonel.

---

[1] *During this scene, the soldiers and officers who were seen scattered from the interlocutors among the tents, little by little come to listen.*
[2] *Dressed as a simple soldier.*

CHARLES.

Father, to a soldier who,
In former battles, sign did give of valor,
It should be given. I would not command,
Nor must, the men who might superior be
In knowledge, skill, and courage than am I.

ANTHONY.

On education is bestowed the rank.

CHARLES.

Accept it, I must not.

ANTHONY.

You would offend
The giver.

CHARLES.

Lincoln, from my brothers, from
Me robbed our independence : tyrants' gifts
I loathe, wish not. Our people have the right
To reward virtue. Lincoln is, as we,
A servant of the country : Congress should,
And not the President, reward the brave.
The power to give reward or penalty
To worthy citizens, or bad, should not
Be delegated to one single man.
The South I do respect ; the North can not
Be free without the freedom of the South.
Assassinate you may, not conquer them.
But are not cursed the Vandals by mankind ?
If to the chariot of this Cæsar, white
Slaves you will drag, new Neros you prepare
For your unhappy children not yet born.
'Gainst the defenders of this Constitution
You wage this war. Your corpses will be stairs
To new Caligulas, and thousand monsters.
You, public treasure rob ; you sap the strength,
And snap the nerve of this great weeping nation.

ANTHONY.

You should not use, nor I permit, such words
Among these tents.

CHARLES.

The sons of freedom should.
To speak I must in my defense. You, father,

And every man or soldier in this camp,
Now have the right to censure me. The truth
No upright man should fear, if tyrants do.
The truth with terror, prison, sword, and death
You wish to silence, forcing us to tremble.
Upon the important war all citizens
To counsel you should call ; it is your duty.
Do I unjustly blame your Lincoln? Then
The laws, the judge, the jury of my country
On me my crime must punish. Here I am.
The yoke of Lincoln do we not endure?
Three years ago, this President most humbly
Did crave the vote from men of humblest mind.
With despotism sends them to fight their brothers,
The very citizens against their will !
If a dictator in the South be wanting,
To free their land from Puritanic war,
And Northern Vandals, this should be the time.
To humble, modest men the Latin Romans,
During the time when Rome was most distressed,
They gave such power ; but they put to death
Any who dared usurp dictatorship.
Jefferson Davis wishes not such power.
Against the Congress, and against us all,
Lincoln is now dictator and a tyrant :
The liberty of speech and of the press
Has e'er the South withheld ? You have; not South.
Without consent of Congress, Lincoln sends
Into bastiles those who tell us the truth ;
And like mad dogs, his myrmidons kill them !
Greenbacks and offices he gives his guards.
Meanwhile, the gold and silver they have robbed
From orphans, widows, are from commerce kept.
Judicial courts are forced to silence. Bought
They have the pulpits. Civil tribunes, martial
Courts by dragoons are kept. Wise men, who speak
Against the monsters, at midnight are dragged
To dungeons from their homes. Their brutal force
Everywhere spreads terror, blood, and death.
Our liberty you kill with your false Union.
You have destroyed with it the rights of man,
And privilege of freedom. Your Augustus,
Lincoln is now proclaimed by Seward ; your
New Anthonius, his Lord and yours. Has he
Not said : " The guns and legions will force you
To vote for him" ?

ANTHONY.

　　　　　Your father, in this camp,
To silence now commands you.　You must take
The loyal oath.　It is your duty, Charles ;
Every soldier has taken it.

　　　　　　　　　　CHARLES.

　　　　　　　　Loyal]|

To whom ?

　　　　　　　　　ANTHONY.

　　To government and President.

　　　　　　　　　CHARLES.]

Of Lincoln, I am not the slave.

　　　　　　　　　ANTHONY.

　　　　　　　　　　It is
But a formality.　We must free slaves.
Of a republic, slavery can never
Be a part.

　　　　　　　　　CHARLES.

　　　　　You for blacks enslave the whites !
Ten millions of white brothers you should not
Exterminate to free four million slaves.
Europe and all the nations who have heard
Your artful argument, and many of us
Who have forgot their country, dear to me,
Regard it, as philanthropy in you.
'Tis a pretext !　To Washington, to Franklin,
Until the present time, you have waged war
Against the Democrats who gave us freedom.
Since that time you have changed your name, but Tories
You were, you are, and will be to the best
Americans.　Although to be, you boast,
The friends of negroes and this country's right,
Tyrants you are to whites and to the blacks.
The Democrats, you know, the worthy sons
Of independence, glorious *rebels* were.
Can you with us now number many *patriots*
As we can find among Confederates ?
You know full well, that with emancipation
You ruin country, constitution, laws ;
And though now both the whites and blacks you ruin,
And with the South the North, you call yourselves
Philanthropists of negro slaves.　You brought

To this distracted land, both war and debts.
The negroes, whom you have already freed,
Do they not suffer in your hands? The thousands
Of helpless beings, oh! bleed or die by want!
If the poor whites have not sufficient work
In these free States, what will you do with three
Or four black millions with enormous debts?
The freedom which you give to them is naught
But a permit to die upon free roads.

ANTHONY.

Has Garibaldi not and Victor Hugo
Praised us for giving freedom to the negroes?

CHARLES.

Such men do wrong to speak of nations they
Know not. Still, we should give no heed to talks
Of daily papers, spread by party spirit.
When Garibaldi, Hugo, and like men
Will hear the craft of Lincoln, Butler, Payne,
They will proclaim that they have been deceived
By the false scribblers who sell mortal lies.

ALPHONSO.

You must now take the oath of loyalty.

CHARLES.

I would die first.

ALPHONSO.

      Always, my friend, you have
Been dear to me. The rigorous command
You know. The General-in-chief wants it.
He gave us the commission and to all:
The same to you. Example of rebellion
You must not give.

CHARLES.

      I've sworn to never swear
For tyrants.

ALPHONSO.

Marshal, Charles must be arrested.

CHARLES.[1]

The first, who does attempt. . . . You will have me
Dead. Alive I will never yield. . . .

[1] *Draws out a revolver.*

ALPHONSO.

In our
Camp, and surrounded by armed men are you.
With pistols thus, dare you provoke your chief?

CHARLES.

Upon my honor, captain, on my country's
Name, oh! do not approach, or I kill you!
Do not, or I kill you!...

ANTHONY.

Oh! Charles, surrender.[1]

SCENE V.[2]

ALPHONSO.

Arrest the murderer alive or dead.
Fire![3]

ALASKA.[4]

On the right. Run, run! Save, save yourself![5]

---

[1] *While the marshal force step toward* CHARLES, *he shoots twice with his revolver. The commandant and an officer fall dead.* CHARLES *runs away. Some other officers and soldiers run after* CHARLES.
[2] *All excepting* CHARLES *and those running after him.*
[3] *Reports of pistols and guns behind the scene.*
[4] *Her voice behind the scene.*
[5] *Musket discharge of a whole company behind the scene.*

ACT IV.

SCENE I.—*A marshal court in the camp of Potomac. Generals, officers, and soldiers coming, and silently going to seats here and there. Lastly,* ANTHONY, ALPHONSO, JUDGE *and* JURY.

ALPHONSO.

The highest trust on us to-day devolves,
Unhappy father.

ANTHONY.

    This situation,
Gen'ral, is cruel, more than death, to me.
I feel now guilty! During all his life!
Charles never gave to me the smallest cause
To reproach him. To me, beloved son
He was : his virtue, honor, spotless habits,
His courage, talents, when my house had peace,
He rendered me the happiest of all fathers.
In New-York, during popular tumult,
From incendiaries, Charles had saved my mansion.
We are his foes ; he knows not how to hate :
For you and me he feels respect. My son
Has acted 'gainst our party with no spite,
If against us. He hopes to save the country
In saving th' independence, and the rights
Of the confederates.

JUDGE.

    He did desert
This camp ; united with the rebel foes :
A colonel, soldiers, officers were killed
By rebels led by him. He killed and wounded
Many, with his own sword, upon the field :
Yea, Colonel Rovellini, had you not
Wounded him, all of us, the Capital
Might be the prey of his intrepid madness.
To hold him prisoner is our great fortune.
If five generals, like Charles, were against us,
We never could subdue such mad rebellion.

Deserters with the penalty of death
Did pay their treason. Justice should be done,
Unless we wish to pay, with our own blood,
Of forbearance the penalty ! Justice,
Severity we are now forced to wield
In these sad times. Prepared is now the court.
Let here the prisoner be now conducted. [1]
Please, Colonel Rovellini, since your son
This camp deserted, how much time may have
Elapsed ?

ANTHONY.

It may now be a month. Since I,
By him, and rebels under him, was conquered,
It is, I think, ten days.

ALPHONSO.

Is coming Charles.

———

SCENE II.

CHARLES,[2] and the Same.

JUDGE.

During the day of the first draft, you are,
Charles Rovellini, here accused to have
Revolted with the mob in New-York 'gainst
The government. With a rebellious mind,
You provoked, with improper language, your
Commanding gen'ral. He ordered the captain
To seize you. But, upon his hesitation,
You, Charles, prevailed. Captain Sebasto was
The first who stepped to do his painful duty ;
The worthy captain at your feet fell dead
By your first shot. Brave soldiers rushed to you.
Two soldiers more you killed, and still two others
Were wounded by your arms : one of them lost
His right foot ; and an arm the second. You
Deserted, Charles, the camp, and saved yourself
By swimming. To the rebel foes united,
Against the loyal States you came. You knew

[1] *A guard retire.*
[2] *Dressed in the uniform of a confederate colonel, with a chain from his left foot to his right wrist. His left arm, suspended by a sling, has a mourning scarf tied to it. He goes to the criminal bench surrounded by armed soldiers.*

Your father was against you, fighting here.
Our mortal foes gave you the rank of colonel.
With sword in hand, and a felonious heart
Of parricidal traitor, you fought us!
Although you are our prisoner, we were
Defeated by the rebels you commanded.
You led the rebels 'gainst your free country . . .

CHARLES.

Free country! 'Tis not free! . . . I beg your pardon.
Such word, from your own mouth, forced me to speak.
But, interrupt your charge is not my wish.
I will now hear, if aught you have to say.

JUDGE.

Only, with painful mind, I ask of you,
If you are guilty of these heinous crimes.

CHARLES.

Of all your accusations, I say nothing.
A false one does offend me much!

JUDGE.

Which is ?

CHARLES.

Never, had I the intent to kill my father.

ANTHONY.

There on the battle-field against me, he,
Himself defended. Slain he might have me ;
Yes ; many times he turned his back from me :
He shouted to his soldiers: *Spare his life !*
Infernal spirits led me to this woe.
In Richmond I might be, had him not wounded.

CHARLES.

I had designed to lead him with my friends
Before the Southern President. I hope
That filial force, my love, and sincere heart
Would have restored to me my dearest father ;
Dearest to me, in spite of hateful party.
I tried to save him from the heinous crime
Of killing his own brothers of the South.

JUDGE.

Have you, Charles Rovellini, nothing else
To say in your defense ?

CHARLES.

You call in me
A crime which I think it my right, the duty
Of a free citizen. This right forced me,
Trembling to shed, against my will, the blood
Of fellow-men in my defense. Yes; 'gainst
Traitors, fanatics of my fatherland,
The South can not their independence gain.
Is not the freedom of the North lost also?
Upon the help which I invoke from Heaven,
Upon my sword I have alone relied,
In helping brothers and the cause of God.
An ignominous death to me don't give:
By like revenge no good to you will come.
You must expect the day of final doom
To thunder near to you, and soon. Against
You all, what I have done is naught of what
I would, to save my brothers and my love.
With you the North can not be free, you Tories
Of our now poor Republic. To the North
You always have been, you are, and will be
Tyrants, unless the Democrats of peace,
In the two sections, shall force you to peace.
Against the noblest citizens you've fought,
During these eighty years of independence.
With crimes you changed your name; but Whigs are Tories.
Without integrity of soul, no man
Has ever been an orator. You rank
With Cicero your Henry Clay, a Whig:
If he, the Roman orator, had been
A gambler, could he now immortal be?
Henry Clay was a Senator of party;
A party orator can not be great,
Has never been, nor he will ever be,
Unless the party weds the truth of God.
God only knows what bitter pangs I feel,
For having killed brave men in my defense.
The war which now you wage against the South
Is not to free black slaves. You had not dared,
During those early days of Lincoln's sway,
To show yourselves as black as you do now,
Against the Constitution, laws, and freedom.
Upon America you now wage war,
And the best citizens of this gone country.
You are sad copies of despotic Cæsar.
When under his dominion, Cæsar wished

To place the Romans, he went 'gainst the Parthians.
Will Lincoln e'er subdue the Northern States,
Unless he first subdue the Democrats,
Who have contended always with his Whigs?
The senators should form the laws in Congress.
If he does not submit, is a mean tyrant,
Traitor, to be condemned to suffer death.
Be it in war or peace, he must consult
The people's will, not his ungoverned mind.
In time of war, against the mother country,
As when in peace, during these eighty years,
All presidents have acted with the people.
The Whig usurper jokes, not executes,
With the consent of people and of God.
His own election, with the gold he gets,
Is buying now from poor and rich, who have
No shame to sell their country's right.   With shots
And terror, he restrains from our free poll,
All timid men, who do not feel this curse.
The chief of freedom should not be the man
Who forces war against the plural vote.
Against our sovereign vote he goes to war,
And laughs at peace: freemen he sends to jail
Without cause, law, nor justice.   Since our glory,
To these three years of woe, three Whigs have been
Elected presidents.   The first was Adams;
The third is joking Lincoln.   Nothing will
I say of Gen'ral Taylor, honest man.
John Adams could do little harm, in times
When Washington was still alive with glory.
As Buonaparte, Lincoln likes to be
An emperor of his country.   John Adams,
With the executive power, when this land
Was reeking sacred blood for independence
And constitution of eight years, could not
Annihilate.   But Lincoln, during times
Of great corruption, many years of party
Dissensions, quarrels, lust, and love of money,
He can now turn this land to crown him Cæsar.
Of the Confederates, the cause is just:
Assassinate you may the South, but then
The curse of God, and nations you shall be
You have already burned their happy lands,
Like Vandals through fair Italy of yore.
To the fanatic Puritans you have
United, trampling under foot the Gospel,
Profaning of the peace our saint Religion,

And preaching from the pulpit to white subjects
Your war-destruction with degraded flags
Upon the sacred towers of the church !
Now that you have suppressed and burnt free press,
Sold editors dispatch invented stories.
Of this pretended justice on the bench,
There sits my father, stained with my own blood,
And I surrounded by armed men, I sick
And chained, am called a traitor of my country !

JUDGE

You stand here, Charles, before this martial court,
To be condemned, if not absolved from death.
You should not us accuse, nor loyal men,
And still more less the President. Your crimes. .

CHARLES.

Of crimes you should not speak, you, the defender
Of robbers, murderers, and incendiaries.
To kill barbarians you call now a crime ?
You have committed crimes of such a brand,
That children, men, the poor of mind, and women,
With terror, now in silence weep, and mourn
These sad calamities. They know full well
That you have no religion, nor e'en faith
In what you say, and never you will have.
By your command your slaves shot me. I had
The right of man defended and the country.
Heaven now permits that I should die your victim.
My body's chained, but my free spirit, never
Will be your slave. You wish my death ; my death
I meet as a free citizen. On earth,
Nor before God would I see you in heaven :
Happy I could not be to see you there.
In my defense, you have forced me to kill
Your slaves ; behold my crime. How can you dare
Now boast th' emancipation of poor negroes,
While the whites, born free, slaves are made by you ?
Better for you, for me, to have no country,
Than be the tyrants of one single soul.
Can you teach freedom with despotic sword ?
You would perform what God has never meant.
The thousands whom you call free negroes now,
They die of misery, and cold, neglected.
White, mutilated slaves, in streets they beg,
In ragged uniform, their daily bread,

Unable to sustain their dying children !
The South kept well their slaves.   What you do now ?
Lo ! blacks and whites by hunger, cold, they die
Under the myrmidons and Butler's rule.
Of war, false reason, yea, the mortal reason
Of ancient times, and ours, from such great crimes
We are absolved.   In vain 't would be for me
To speak against inveterate abuse,
Sophism, war laws.   Those whom we kill in war,
By you, by me, by emp'rors, are no crimes ?
When true religion and th' Almighty's science,
True knowledge shall have taught to men, for which
We breathe this mortal mission, then posterity
Will call the war a crime of ancient powers,
A crime of present nations !   Call it duty,
As you please : though on earth the stronger law
Is flattered by false priests and false divines,
The Almighty's judgment we shall hear in heaven ;
We shall be forced to listen to His laws.
When North's invaders shall receive from God
The shafts of retribution, God will crown
The martyrs of the South on earth, in heaven.
I am accused by you for killing men
In self-defense, when from this camp I ran
To save my life and honor from your crimes ;
When you forced me to murder brother Abel !
I ran from base aggressors, brutal Cains,
To moral Abels, who defend their rights :
I ran for aiding those whom you insulted.
I should be criminal as you, had I
With you united, to force them to your
Horrible Union.   At the head of my
Dear friends, I came to fight assassins, Whigs
Uncivilized, without humanity .
My fate wished father mortal foe to me.
Under his sword I fell.   The sun was setting ;
I lost my senses.   When returned to life,
Horror I felt to see myself thus guarded
By mortal foes, and father by my bed.

JUDGE.

The virtues of your father can not save you,
After what you have said against this court
And government.   You fought against that flag.

CHARLES.

The stains which you have made upon that flag,
The virtues of the children not yet born
Can never cleanse and make it what it was.
That flag was bright before these last three years.
Upon the fun'ral-pile of my dear country,
I now must die. Were there a tyrant only,
This hand would have attempted its own duty :
But, Lincoln dead, would Hamlin there be better ?
Upon the ground should fall too many heads :
This shame can not blot out one single Brutus.
You call the South rebellious ! Who rebelled
Against this government if not yourselves ?
Have you not sent fanatics to the South
With never-ending diatribes on the slaves,
And never-ending speeches in the Senate ?
Has not been caned Charles Sumner in the Senate ?
Was not John Brown in old Dominion sent ?
Have you not sanctified the Puritan ?
The South secedes, because you them insulted ;
The South secedes, because first you rebelled ;
The South secedes, because you shot them first ;
The South secedes, because you brought the tariff
Worse than it was in time of English mother.
The noblest fathers of the Revolution
Were born from South. Great Lee is not alone.
Could you subdue the sons of noble South,
Forced we should be to mourn the nation's death.

JUDGE.

You have already heard his fell intentions,
His crimes in this rebellious, tottering country.
The jury must now give impartial judgment.
Many deserters have been shot to death
By the law. Charles Rovellini, a traitor
And rebel, is arraigned for many murders.
Against the loyal government he came,
And loyal father, heading mortal foes.
This martial court he did insult ; we are
And government by him insulted. Had
He had the chance presented, he would have
Assassinated President Lincoln.
The law condemns the traitor to be hung.
The country asks of you to judge, now only,
If Charles is innocent or guilty. Merely
We pray you, do not lose much time ; be quick ;
The court is waiting here your loyal judgment.[1]

[1] *The Jury retires.*

SCENE III.

Silence.

SCENE IV.

Jury, and the Same.

JURY.

We judge him guilty.

JUDGE.

On this afternoon,
At two o'clock, Charles Rovellini, you,
As a rebellious traitor, shall be hung.

ANTHONY.[1]

Your pardon in this paper, Charles, is written,
If you submit to one condition.

CHARLES.

What?

ANTHONY.

If now against the rebels you will arm,
Here is your pardon with a Gen'ral's rank.

CHARLES.

The pardon of my God I hope to get ;
My brow with pardon, Lincoln shall not brand.
When but a child, to me the Roman deeds,
With Jesus morals, you were teaching, father ;
To me your language was sublime ! Shall I,
I, for this life, wage war now to my brothers ?

ANTHONY.

My noble son, oh ! you have conquered me !
Upon my withered cheeks you see my tears !
More than myself, my son, I do love you.
Oh ! my dear Charles, the government and party

[1] *Coming forward and taking a paper from his portfolio.*

Have you condemned ; but I can not, oh ! never !
Oh ! pardon ! Your great virtues conquered me.
To you, I feel myself, by far, inferior.
The dreadful thought of having wounded you,
When you so nobly did defend yourself,
Soon will bring me to my now open grave !
I am a most unhappy father, Charles,

CHARLES.

As well as we, usurpers must die, father.
Cursed are the graves of tyrants : bathed with tears
And blessed with holy prayer is the just.

SCENE V.

CHARLOTTE *and* ALASKA—*Same.*

CHARLES.

Dear mother, sister ! As I have told you,
A death most horrible I must now die.
One Lincoln's pardon is in father's hands,
If I, with rank of gen'ral, will now go
To war against my brothers. What say you ?

CHARLOTTE.

Die !

CHARLES.

What say you, Alaska ?

ALASKA.

I say, die !
I know my brother was not born for shame.

CHARLES.

Happy I will now die, since I can say :
You, dear, have always been my pride. Oh ! come
You both to my sad heart. Sob not. Leave me
To die like a brave soldier. I selected,
Before you came, the death you counsel me.
To bless your family come here, dear father.[1]

Anthony goes to them. Father and son fall into each other's arms.

ACT V.

SCENE I.

Prison near the Camp of Potomac.

CHARLES. THOMPSON.

THOMPSON.

From the first day of our birth, my friend, we
All, upon earth, are on the road to Heaven.
You have few moments of this mortal life.
Your happiness or your eternal loss
Is now depending on your holy creed,
Which in that book you have.   Upon this Bible,
Holy precepts gives God.   In duty bound,
We must believe, we all, his great commands.
Without this Christian faith, you can not enter
That blessed kingdom.   God to Moses gave
This book, and Jesus Christ, with his own blood,
Our human race redeemed.

•   CHARLES.

                  You, with that book,
Many of your divines have wronged this country.
Our citizens should never have permitted
False preachers of the Gospel.   Our grandfathers,
When they these laws of freedom had decreed,
Left to their children a free conscience also,
Without intolerance, your censure, sway.
On earth our greatest duty ought to be
That of true citizens.   Unchristian, false
Ambition of this earth and heaven, you have.
Of Satan are your acts and prayer.   You,
Reformers, bad as popes you blame.   You blame
All learned men, professors contradicting
Your talk against the light of God, of Nature.
Teachers dare not to demonstrate the laws

Of God, of great Creation, of the Stars,
Of Galileo the science with such popes
Reformed. Astronomy, geology,
Nor of great Newton you respect the logic.
You scorn the popes, but you are popes reformed
Against the science, arts, theatres, dance,
Nature's instruction, and the will of God :
Against the will of God and very Gospel !
Your doctrine is all worldly pride and money.
When you compare creation with the Bible,
Naught is God's work. Infinity is naught,
Nothing the laws of Nature with your talk.
In these unhappy States, you are the cause
Of our calamities and ruin. Your preaching
Has wronged this country more than popes in Spain,
In Italy, or France. Here we have not
An inquisition of the middle age,
With dungeons, fire, monks ; but here we have
A moral inquisition, still more fatal
Than Europe had, because the Puritans
And monks reformed surpass the papal monks
In number, cruelty, fanaticism,
In spite of God's instruction and man's wisdom.
The men of science, you condemn the wise,
Because philosophy reveals the truth :
The truth can not corrupt. Your impious deeds
From ignorance are sprung and crafty boast.
You call it blasphemy when scholars say
That light is emanated from the sun,
Because the Bible says : The light God did
Create upon the first day. You have preached
Against wise men, who can not hold such views
As you. When under ground my bones shall be,
You also will curse me. In church have you
Not cursed most honest men in life and death,
After you robbed their bread ? Beyond his grave
You cursed Girard, and held his college, left
By testament, before his death, to God's
Science, professors, not divines, nor priests.
College and church you turn to your own profit.
You slander science, arts, and benefactors;
You seem not to believe what you profess.

THOMPSON.

I see in you the school of Paine, Voltaire ;
But when before th' Almighty will appear....

CHARLES.

Few moments of this life remain to me ;
On such a subject to dispute is useless ;
It would excite us both, without conviction.
To most profound reflection, Doctor, leave,
Pray, leave me here alone.

THOMPSON.

May Heaven now do
For your immortal soul, what I can not.

CHARLES.

I now am on the way where all are brothers :
Here, on this earth, in this precarious life,
Many of us, called friends, in secret strive
To cheat the noblest of their Christian neighbors,
To please the tyrants of the land ; but there,
In that immortal life, where the black vail
Of ignorance is rent, the truth is bright
On God's rewarded, blessed souls of Heaven.

SCENE II.

CHARLES.

Of immortality I am not certain !
Th' annihilation of my soul with horror
My mind oppresses ! E'en this very being,
Thought, ardent wish to follow virtue, filial
Love, patriotic heart, sublime devotion
For dear Virginia, lofty thoughts of heaven . . .
Oh ! shall I lose the whole, and be as once,
Before this troubled life, so brief with tears ?
To lose this light forever, and the hope
Of future life as a reward of virtue,
For which I felt a blessing in my grief. . . .
The stars, the sun, the planets, God's creation,
Infinity ! To study flowers, herbs,
The knowledge of this earth adorned with birds,
Fish, animals, and men. I have not learned
Yet of our God his silent daily teaching.
If sent for progress on this earth are we,
It would be wrong with God to blot us out

From His almighty presence, when we feel
And just begin his great Divine instruction,
With hope of immortality.... What justice
Receives the good without reward in Heaven?....
Oh! come, Virginia, to this anxious heart!

SCENE III.

Virginia,[1] *and the Same.*

CHARLES.

Do let me hear once more thy dear, sweet voice.
Such sobbing! Oh! thy gasping breath unmans me!
Shall I no more upon this earth hear thee?
From thy sweet lips is gone the heavenly smile,
For which I felt the life of bliss, of God!
Shall we not meet in Heaven?

VIRGINIA.

Can—you—Charles, doubt?
The Son of God, our Saviour Christ, who came
Into this world, tells us, by his own words,
We are immortals. Oh! my faith is sure!

CHARLES.

Are these not brutes among the cruel Christians?
Dearest, I would believe all that you do!
Than other nations, Christians are not better,
This civil war has shown them worse than tigers,
Are there not women bearing Christian names,
And false divines in church, who now applaud
Assassins, thieves, felonious deeds, and arson?
They give to black slaves arms : the beasts renew
The shame and degradation of Domingo.

VIRGINIA.

My father, brothers have been killed : the home
Of my own birth, the cheerful garden, flowers,
And library are now reduced to ashes.
But yesterday, my mother died in tears,
By want, in rags, and in my arms! On earth

[1] *In mourning dress.*

Nothing remains to me but tears and mourning.
The Vandals have condemned you, Charles, to die!
Still, these calamities I will endure
With resignation, ordered by our faith,
Rememb'ring Jesus' passion, and the cross.
Do you the same.   On your salvation think˙:
Heed not oppressors who possess no faith.

CHARLES.

Have you the dagger which you promised me?

VIRGINIA.

Here, near my heart—'tis sharp.   Oh! I repent
Of having promised it to you!

CHARLES.

What for?

VIRGINIA.

A soul immortal have you not?

CHARLES

I hope.

VIRGINIA.

Are you not certain?

CHARLES.

Dearest, I must not
And would not you deceive. I hope. This wish,
This warm desire, which God gave me, I feel,
I burn for immortality. This hope
Is almost certainty. Celestial hope
I've felt of an immortal life, since I've
Loved you, since with your love you honored me:
But, hope is not a certainty. Too sure
I am of this repulsive death before me;
Certain I am of your dear love, Virginia;
I am not certain of a life beyond
The grave, a life not yet begun—unknown!

VIRGINIA.

You make me shudder! You can not be saved
Without a childlike faith in the Redeemer!

CHARLES.

Such blind belief keeps all the Christians slaves.
The certain truths of nature's science, arts,
Clear demonstrated like geometry,
Are what we must believe. Had God forbid
Untrammeled thought upon the works of nature,
A tyrant he would be. He has created
For man's progress these wondrous works around.
The popes, the bishops of reform could not
Rule us, nor human beasts, were we instructed
As God has always wished and daily shows.
The source of all the mortal evils is
This very blind belief! Enlightened people
Have never been enslaved by priests nor kings.
Had not this country been enslaved by this
Belief of yours, the Whigs and Puritans
Could not succeed to cheat and rule us all!
The Cæsars or usurpers of this land
United were with clergy and the church,
Who kept in blind belief the poor of mind
In fear of an invented hell hereafter.
Are not their very deed deserving hell?
I hope just punishment will be given
By God to these usurpers of my land.

VIRGINIA.

To God, the King of kings, we must submit.
Yea, naught we have to lose when we believe
That which the Gospels teach.

CHARLES.

           The Gospels be,
Not all divines should we believe. The Son
Of God was poor, and poor he died : divines
In gilded churches preach, and wish us not
To think, but with their mind. We are by God
Instructed night and day, by his great work,
Infinity of stars, of planets, suns,
With animals on earth and in the sea.
To scan the sky we are by God invited ;
The tyrants, fearing God's instruction, tell
These false divines to blind with sophisms Christians.
The rights of man, the study of nature's works,
Is true religion by the Lord accepted.
All civil discords are originated

From these religions, now so much divided.
The one with senseless commentaries cites
The Bible ; th' other with controversies,
Polemics start dissents in church and home :
Thus trampling under foot the common-sense
And the divine precepts of Christ, they preach
Treason to God, and quereles never ending.
The dirk, Virginia. . . .

VIRGINIA.

          To reward in heaven
Your virtues, God awaits ; but, self-murder,
Charles, is by God, most solemnly, forbid.

CHARLES.

'Gainst my will I'm now forced to kill myself.
Could I escape, I would. You see these chains !
I hope . . . It seems to me the heavenly love
I feel for you and for our country, can
Not terminate. I feel my soul immortal.

VIRGINIA.

This world has been for you but grief ; for me
Has been a world of tears. Our glory must,
Will be, my dear, in heaven.

CHARLES.

          Give me the dirk.
If you deny it me, soon on a scaffold,
Oh! like a criminal, they will hang me !
Such ignomiulous death is most horrible.

VIRGINIA.

This mortal night must have for us an end !

CHARLES.

A dreadful dream is this, my dearest love.

VIRGINIA.

I should have been too happy had our God
Permitted me to be your bride on earth !

CHARLES.

In heaven you will be mine for evermore.

VIRGINIA.

Betrothed we are to mourn, to weep, and die.

CHARLES.

When on the day I first saw you, I felt
A new existence. Such existence was
A new, celestial life. This love of heaven,
I hope in God will always be with me :
It can not die with mortal body. You,
With love, to that eternal sphere lead me,
To God's religion. These divines, these priests
Of reformation have kept me from God.

VIRGINIA.

Do listen to the Gospel ; pardon all
These base fanatics and these false divines.[1]

CHARLES.

'Tis the last moment of my life. Give me,
Oh ! quick, the dirk. The door will open now.
Shall I now suffer ignominious death ?

VIRGINIA.[2]

Oh ! why does my religion now forbid me
To follow thee? Accept, O clement God !
Our sacrifice !

CHARLES.

       Upon this earth my last
Kiss, dearest, be this. God, I hope, will us
Unite in that eternal sphere.[3] A black
Vail is before my eyes. . . . Do . . . leave . . .the blood
To flow. . . .

VIRGINIA.

       Upon the earth this precious blood,
Charles, oh! I can not see ! Unearthly force
I feel in me ! All, all is lost on earth ![4]
Our sacrifice, this martyrdom, Oh, God !
Thou canst not punish. Charles, thou art my God.
Oh ! heaven is not unjust ! But if perdition

---

[1] *The clock strikes two.*
[2] *After giving the dirk, she prostrates herself on the floor.*
[3] *He wounds himself.*
[4] *She rises from the sofa with the bloody dirk in her hand*

Opens to thee, to me . . . I must. The Lord
Wishes me now to come to thee. Yes, dear
'Twill be to me to suffer there with thee !
Oh ! this warm blood ! Our home is there, my love.
To heaven I'll follow thee. [1]

SCENE IV.

ANTHONY, CHARLOTTE, ALASKA—*Same.*

CHARLOTTE.

My son ! The blood . . .
It bursts from both their hearts !

ALASKA.

Oh ! with my brother,
My sister dear expires ! [2]

ANTHONY.

My son ; oh ! pardon
Your father most unhappy!

CHARLES.

With her dear
Smile, father, mother, look, Alaska, she . . .
The spirit . . . of Virginia . . . beckons . . . me . . .
To . . . heaven! We . . . there . . . will . . . meet . . . for . . ever! [3]

ANTHONY.

This is
The just reward of stolid love of party !
With this dear son, I lost my country's freedom!

[1] *She wounds herself.*
[2] VIRGINIA *dies in the arms of* ALASKA.
[3] *He expires.*

www.ingramcontent.com/pod-product-compliance
Lightning Source LLC
Chambersburg PA
CBHW022151090426

42742CB00010B/1468